The Mirror Tent

Gerard Smyth

ACKNOWLEDGEMENTS

Acknowledgments are due to the editors of the following publications where many of these poems, or versions of them, first appeared: *Agenda, An Sionnach* (Creighton University Press, USA), *Best of Irish Poetry 2007, Cork Literary Review, Cyphers, Irish Pages, New Hibernia Review* (University of St. Thomas, USA), *Poetry Review, Poetry Ireland Review, Poetry Salzburg Review, The Irish Examiner, The Irish Times, The SHop, The Stinging Fly, Something Beginning with P, Southword, Studies, Sunday Miscellany Anthology, The Warwick Review, Waxwing Poems* and *Wingspan: a Dedalus Sampler.*

Some poems also appeared in translation, in Spanish in *Clarín* (Buenos Aires), and in Polish in *New Writers' Press Antologia* (Poland). 'He Who Treads the Boards' originally appeared in a different draft, under the title 'Thespian', on the Department of Foreign Affairs cultural website, *E-Zine.* 'An Evening Walk in Maryland' was written as a collaboration with the artist Donald Teskey for Poetry Ireland's Rhyme and Resin exhibition. Several of these poems were also broadcast on *Sunday Miscellany* on RTÉ Radio 1.

*for my sister Anne
and in memory of our parents
Bridget and Laurence Smyth*

Contents

THREE

FOUR

ONE

Riddles and Orisons

to the memory of Jack Hoey, teacher

Straight-backed, arms outflung.
In front of everyone
he stood like a singer about to sing
his favourite aria.
The dust of school-chalk
lay on his shoulders.

He read with both eyes closed,
brooded over Matthew Arnold
and Samuel Coleridge
during the last lesson of the day
when in a voice that was ceremonious
he created the atmosphere of the Lakes
just by saying *Windermere.*

Shakespeare, Yeats,
Father Hopkins, Soldier Ledwidge.
On afternoons when the glinting sun
came in or rain fell hard
on the window-ledge
he made their riddles and orisons
rise from the page.

In the Bakery

I sliced the round fruit down to the core,
a tight knuckle that tasted sour.
Good hands lined with flour
were creating something beautiful
out of the dough, beating it flat.

Silence is golden, someone sang on the old radio
that used to fade and then come back.
It was almost a biblical task:
taking from the oven the abundance
of the baker's dozen: soda farls, apple tarts,
wheaten bread with a crust of thickness.

It was a place of sifting fingers
and measuring vessels, of work
that became a ritual when I filled
and emptied the kiln
or gathered up egg shells and apple skins.

Picturehouse

The Brides of Dracula,
Jason and the Argonauts.

In the picturehouse on Sunday,
with our lucky bags and ticket stubs,
we sat in the ranks of the hypnotised.
Those who believed in the divine
transfiguration of false idols.

All of us close together in a dark hush,
lulled by the first arpeggios
of a menacing theme. The plush red seats
made us kings and queens.
The projector beam was like light

from a beacon when the scalloped curtain
rose up or parted to reveal
a cinematic vista: Piccadilly and all its neon.
Tumbleweed rolling in tufts
down a lonely Main Street.

Same Old Crowd

Once a year we gather to reminisce
on things that happened, things that didn't.
Together we are a reunion of shadows

huddled around a table of drinks;
the occasion on which again we are part
of the same old crowd.

Each is his own biographer,
each the maker of his own folklore and myth.
There is one who remembers

and one whose memories have been eclipsed
by disillusionment and the passage
of years since our initiations

in fellowship, high-spiritedness,
the antics of youth; since first we heard
Into the Mystic, slow-danced to *Hey Jude.*

The Cana Inn

The law did not like the long hair
of the cider-drinkers, the ones who made the din
on Saturday night in The Cana Inn.

Not the one in Galilee, the Cana
of the wedding feast and the water-to-wine miracle.
But the one they later knocked to rubble

off Grafton Street. It was where we revelled,
carelessly dressed in denim and corduroy,
equipped with copies of Kerouac.

It was the end of summer, the waning
of another decade. The jukebox played
a voice with gravitas: it was Johnny Cash
singing *Girl from the North Country.*

Homage to Hartnett

From Granada he brought back
Lorca's gipsy ballads.
When the blackbird whistled
in the school-hedge hedges
of Croom and Camas
he was there to listen, a naturalist,
a new and living Ó Rathaille.

In Kensington, on the underground
where nobody looks at anyone else
he looked ascetic
like a young Jean Paul Belmondo
as bony as the Rock of Skellig.

And on Leeson Street,
in the Saturday crowd he was there again,
raising a glass, striking a match:
the haiku-master of Emmet Road
wedged between Sweet Afton
and Woodbine smoke.

i.m. Jerome Hynes

Tears have a history of falling
Galway Kinnell says in his poem 'Goodbye'.
But it was the history of a smile you taught us.
How it lives, how it dies.

We have just come from Vinegar Hill
to hear the opera singers sing,
alone and in unison, an autumnal aria
from *Lucia di Lammermoor.*

And we shall miss the way you stood,
dressed up, black suited, colour
on your cheeks in the doorway of the theatre
where you were ready to give your salute

and greeting, your handshake
that gripped each of us in turn
as we paraded one by one
into the audience waiting for the overture.

John Field

Born beneath cathedral bells,
he heard their morning and evening *Pathetique.*
The cheerfulness of their clanging metals
came gusting to his doorstep.

The boy from Golden Lane
with an ear for melancholy.
The idol of Paris, Vienna, St. Petersburg.
The pensive maker of the transcendent nocturne.

Moscow congratulated him
for his lullabies to soothe the nineteenth century.
Night after night the privileged and prosperous
came to hear and applaud

John Field who made piano-chords
sound like the rise and fall of breath,
who when he played seemed to bend
and whisper to his easeful melody.

Visiting Chopin's Heart

At the end of his life he called for
a cup of Pyrenees water
to cleanse his heart, prepare it for
its final prelude: the homecoming to Warsaw,

a city built from ruins
and in the middle of it Chopin's heart.
The rest of Chopin lies in Père Lachaise,
beside Michel Petrucciani,
another pianist, whose night-prayer was jazz:
the dusky ballads.

Chopin the émigré never forgot
the grandfather clock that let time pass
more slowly; or the spring thaw
in the woodland his father bought—
ice snapping in a short recital
of nocturne and sonata.

Relic

Through Drogheda's streets she took me to see
the head of Oliver Plunkett
in close-up so close his expression was vivid
and scary to a child who still believed
all he was told.

His lips were sealed and his eyes closed
in the shut reliquary. I thought if he could speak
his voice would be authoritative, stern:
a paradigm of human goodness, a guide
for weaker men.

Through Drogheda's streets she led me
into a place of supplicants
contemplative in the way they stood
and looked at the head of Oliver Plunkett
who looked like he was listening.

To Bobrowski

All the essential poems are in your book
and in your landscape of *heart-mysteries.*
We passed through it: the swathes
of forest greenwood,
alder paths, rivers carrying the ashes
of great wars and ruined cities.

We passed through it on the autobahn
from which we saw the wind-farms
of new Germany. Their great mills spinning
in a spiritual dance.

Jan Palach

It was a beautiful evening with friends
at the table, but then
an image flared into my head.
It was one of sacrificial immolation:
Jan Palach who died to light the dark.

I remember seeing imprinted on the page
the student martyr
with the melancholy gaze.

The man-child in the photograph
who went where he had to go
into the conflagration
that sometimes is the only light we have.

On Grodska Street

Out through the door of the Baroque church
come the big organ-notes of a cantata
that send pigeons fluttering between pillars.
Then the exodus of Bach-worshippers.

There must be an aphrodisiac in the summer heat
these hot nights in Hotel Senacki
on Grodska Street. We are up in the attic
wondering whether this was ever
a place of secret confabulation in the Cold War days
or during the jackboot occupation.

In a room with the blinds down, the electric fan
going full blast, we hear around us
the overlapping sounds of horse and carriage,
paternosters, and the evening bells of Krakow.

Museum of Last Things

Where the trains arrived
there is a stillness you can watch
in the heat haze and in the snow rain.

It would be easy to say
that this is a place without nature;
that would be wrong.

There is hair that lived on
when shaved from the head.
Anonymous tresses, braids and bobs

stored in the museum of last things
where nothing is forgotten.
Suitcases without luggage,

spectacle frames in a tangled knot.
A midden of possessions relinquished
like the last strength

of Maximilian Kolbe,
the last strength of those who entered
beneath the false promise.

In Vilnius

They are all radiance, the brides of Vilnius.
It seems as if Saturday is one long wedding.
Brides stepping through the Gate of Dawn,

couples being photographed next to Mickiewicz
or under the sign for the road to Minsk.
They go slowly into the Church of St. Casimir

and into the long-standing edifice
where frescoes come back to life,
the church that Napoleon wanted to carry to Paris.
The one he turned into a bed for his horse-cavalry.

To a Latvian Poet

He stands like a sentinel.
His ruddy complexion and snow beard
make me think of Rembrandt's
ancient sitters.

He speaks quietly and we listen
to his early life: his seven winters
of exile from Riga for being in league
with the academy of treason.

But that was long ago
when the birds of Latvia refused to sing.
Today he is the honoured poet
who seeks not to be noticed

even when he is called by name
to step forward into the circle
to read a poem that transcribes
his noble nature.

Folktale

The war was on; the land of the lotus
was nailed to the cross.
You were not yet born,
not yet nurtured in Asian etiquette,
when Christmas bombs were falling on Hanoi,
when every day was more of the same
on the Ho Chi Minh trail.

And now in this far country,
that was to be a *tabula rasa*
for those we named *the boat people,*
your father still hands on
memories, stories, a patriotic song:
all that he remembers long after
the long war ended with a war's crescendo.

Ostend

We took the nightboat to Ostend,
Hotel Magritte with its *art deco* décor.
The beeswax glaze of the wooden floor
reflected your gipsy skirt
and the brass buttons of the concierge.

On the first evening we walked
to where the North Sea knocked on the sea-wall,
a wall as thick as the walls of Limerick.

In silk kimonos and feather boas
young women in the brothel district
idled in windows that were like pavilions
of unblemished flesh: they uttered nothing
but gave us looks that we brushed against

on the way to a late-night discotheque
in rain that was unceasing, indefatigable;
black North Sea rain like shards of shrapnel.

Nora Barnacle's House

I was looking for Nora Barnacle's house
but never found it.
Instead I saw her apparition in the water
with the Corrib swan,
the one leading the others forward,
the one with slender contours
eyeing the stranger on the riverbank
under the flowering tree.

I was looking for the house of Nora Barnacle
but wandered instead up the aisle
of the stone-walled cathedral,
where liturgical smoke lingered
after some ritual, after the sign of peace
when everyone leaves to go out
into the other world where first
their eyes adjust and then they see
the choppy Corrib, the swan in the water,
and between the branches of the tree
petals falling, settling
on the grassy bank beside the weir.

TWO

Survivors

My father knew them, the master-brewers
of Rainsford Street who watched
and learned their father's trade
in malt and barley, hops and yeast.
Now they are gone with all their secrets
and old ways of tossing the grain.

My father knew them, the menders
of broken shoes, the brotherhood
of men with joiner's tools and the sailors
home from sea, who rose at noon.
Some were the forgotten of the Great War,
survivors who saw Edward Thomas's

Avenue without end. My father knew them
in their supping places, canal-barge pilots
who navigated seven locks,
the newsboys of Inchicore and Kilmainham
whose evening mantra announced
the final score, the fall of nations.

Draper's Window

in Francis Street

There were armfuls of cloth in clear divisions:
cotton, linen, the new synthetics;
winding reams with curled-up edges
in the draper's window
and down the full length of the shop.

Fabrics of conspicuous and flamboyant colours
that would look good when cut
and stitched and pieced together
by women working the treadles and wheels
of Singer sewing machines.

It was a jumbled bazaar of curtain lace,
Communion veils. The cloth merchant
knew his trade: spotless white
for the soon-to-be-bride, lavender shades
for the widow tired of blacks and greys.

All That is Left ...

All that is left of the medieval wall stands over
the underground river that snakes beneath
Fishamble, Cornmarket, Winetavern Street
where we strolled together like the pair in the legend
of Diarmuid and Gráinne or stopped to stand in
from the rain that fell on the ghosts of Hibernia.
The orators and the uncrowned king: all the fallen
who rose again on the stonemason's plinth.

In the Castle yard a tourist camera clicks, makes an image
of the gates through which the English departed.
In Ship Street walls were built on the bones of men.
Walls that listen to what the grey gulls tell.
The tourist can smell the lapidary damp
and puddled rain behind the Centre of Administration.

An Evening Walk in Maryland

When my father was a tired old man,
his pride in the Republic gone,
every evening he went for a walk in Maryland,
stood by the canal or stopped
at the dry fountain in James's Street.

By way of crumbling lane and convent wall,
gothic spire and brewery chimney,
he ambled as far as his last glimpse of the Liffey
before it disappeared to appear again
at Islandbridge and Chapelizod.

When my father became a tired old man,
coping with the scarcity of divine help,
each night he emptied his pocket of its hoard
of coins and his betting docket for the horse
and jockey that tumbled in the final furlong.

Hartmann's Camera

It was the year of *yeah, yeah, yeah*
and hair the length of Christ's.
The ambling horse,
a dray-nag pulling a laden cart
through the centre of the metropolis,
must have been one of the last.

In Erich Hartmann's snaps of Dublin 1964
I see again my father's city of lore:
small boats on the river
and people crossing the bridges,
all weary like the gravediggers
who have shovelled earth

for a burial in the boneyard.
I see again my father's city
of bad old days that were better by far.
Broken ground and jutting chimneys:
his whole universe that vanished
through the aperture of Hartmann's camera.

Written from Memory

How much of memory
is imagination? – Linda Pastan

The street we came from has disappeared
and the people too have vanished
into nostalgia, reminiscence, a lament for the past:
the milk-wagon, the baker's van,
the dull clang of a convent bell
striking twelve and six o'clock.
And the doleful Sundays with their
three-o'clock spill of men from the pub.
There was parleying on the corner,
small talk, racing tips. It was closing time,
the post-meridian hour of ease.
They were men who looked crumpled,
dressed in the livery of their Sunday wardrobe.
Sometimes they stood under the rain
with our fathers and uncles
arguing for hours about Cassius Clay.
Each of them wanting the last word
before going home to their soft armchairs.
Over dinner they'd say nothing.
Sometimes it was wise to be taciturn.

Cinéma Vérité

It happened in the style of cinéma vérité:
Downriver to the bridge before the bay
the Liffey barges brought black porter.
That was when the poet with the black fedora
passed this way through the city he loved.

Wearing the aura of a Celtic monk,
his coat, a solid garment, buttoned up,
his walk of contemplation took him
to places we still behold: Merchant's Arch,
old St Weburgh's where pigeons on the ledges
listen to Protestant bells: the call to morning service
and, later, the call to vespers.

Old Haunts

Old haunts are best.
So you take the bus as far as the vestiges
of the city walls, the malt-and-barley district,
place of your first oracles.
To where the bells chime in the evening,
and bellringers ache in the Dean's cathedral.
Old haunts are best. The forty steps,
the tavern of shifting dust
where Napper Tandy plotted sedition.
The whiff of Liffey sediment,
risen from the riverbed, hangs over the market
of second-hand shoes, cast-off coats;
things discarded but still of use to the salvager.
In the office where our city fathers
fill the document baskets, the chill
goes out of the day. This is The Pale
and here are the keg-yards shut away
in the neighbourhood built on mud foundations.
It is where Lord Iveagh bestowed his favours:
the parks and gardens, red-brick mansions,
the bathhouse cold as Alaska.

Eccles Street

It was the silver age of the sepia print.
From Eccles Street
the wanderer set out in the heat of June,
to take the epic route,

to make a day of small detours
with cronies in the meeting rooms
and hostelries.
Journey-man. Pilgrim. Tenant
of a creaky house

that after slow decline was gone in time,
I retrace your path
from the precinct of the dispossessed
to the dunes in Sandymount

and the round Martello with its climbing
steps and assonant echoes
that echo still, a hundred years since
Odysseus prowled his Dublin streets
and bawdy-house.

Nostalgia for the World

Today I went looking
among the loved ones
to find my long-dead parents' grave,
to find where they are wedded
in that lasting marriage
of dust to dust, ashes to ashes.

In Mount Jerome
at the end of the long entrance avenue
I sensed on all sides
nostalgia for the world,
and the end of time
for the just and unjust.

Those who were elders
and those in the flower of youth.
Generation after generation
in the maw of hardened clay,
the east wind creeping up on them
and the thundercloud that brings its cabaret.

Dollars

Grandmother never allowed the electric in
because it was that fearful thing
that killed her son in America.

The boy who sent back dollar bills,
who in his stiff white collar
and antique tweeds looked down on us
from the cherrywood frame,
his place of honour.

Grandmother became a book
of bewilderment after the bad news
appeared in the long-distance telegram,
a message that remained for years

on the big open dresser
with its rows of cups, like commas,
its brimming jugs with rustic scenes.
And higher up on the dresser's peaks
she kept the dollars out of reach.

Ancestral Place

Leaving the drumlins
for the ploughland of Meath
we passed on the way the ancestral place.
The green gate, the roof
that needs mending if it is to be saved.

Roof of straw, house at the cross.
Rusting spade, rusting fork.
Worms in the wood
of the ladder that reached to the top
of the haycock with its wide summer girth
and scattering seed.

From the chimney breast
that held it for years, soot falls,
descending like wrath.
Forgotten grass grows in the yard
where we built a pyre
of blankets, bedsheets, aprons, oilcloth:

possessions that reeked
of damp bottom drawers
and the quotidian heat of the big open fire
that was constant but changed
from summer furnace to winter cradle.

Dreamsong

The dead from family photographs
appeared again in a dream I had.
Not everyone, just those from the farm
wanting their old lives back.

In the dream I saw again the boy I was
that boyhood August
with grandmother feeding the calves
and strolling the yard, her strong arms
holding ingots of turf,
her hair pinned up in an old woman's bun.

The half-door on its hinges
sagged and screeched. The hens
were going asleep in their beds of straw,
their safehouse of feathers and shit.

Under the Brigid's Cross
she murmured her Hail Marys,
conjured butter from buttermilk.
Then wrapped it in a muslin cloth.

Once, on Long Island ...

*...we wept and talked about leaving
and never left.*
– Kapka Kassabova

Once on Long Island, on a day of leaf-smoke
rising, at the end of an ocean drive,
I came to a house that was like the home
of Jimmy Stewart in *It's A Wonderful Life*.

I was among three generations assembled
for an afternoon tea ceremony.
The octogenarian who sat beside me
took me through a long family narrative

that started on the fertile plain
and ancient roads of Slane and Tara.
From the year of her departure

she unlocked a big portmanteau of recollections
that started with a rooming house in America,
and long avenues with their sidewalks of destiny.

From the Archive

From early footage, they smile at us.
Greybeard fathers, strapping sons.
Prospectors in a foreign land, fortune-seekers
in the costumes of their era: waistcoats, collarless shirts.

You just know that theirs was a hard-luck story;
that they never completed the inner journey
of their hearts but instead were slaves
to the ganger, slaves to the Manor Lord.

From shaky footage, they smile at us,
shopgirls who on Sunday took long walks
with others who crossed on the emigrant route,
bringing their St Christophers, their dancing shoes.

THREE

Cool of the Day

It was an evening for the mowing of lawns,
the clipping of hedgerows.
Not staying indoors
with the soap opera, the idiots' quiz
or watching CNN
for news of the next apocalypse.

My companion was sitting in bluejeans,
in the walled garden,
sipping a Burgundy
that was close to a menstrual colour,
enjoying the best weather in weeks,
the indolent heat of an Indian summer.

Her face has always been the iconography
of my best dreams: my gladness,
my rapture, my golden apple.
In the walled garden she was chatting away,
her necklace of pearls—
the mother-to-daughter heirloom she wears—
as cool as the cool of the day.

Surrender

Your old dress of full-length chiffon
hangs like the ghost of Emily Dickinson,
forlorn in our backroom.

The room is one we seldom enter.
It prompts memories of an evening
at the proms, a day in Ravenna.

It is here that we consign
to the rag-heap and the jumble pile
your glamour frocks, my tweeds

as thick as body-armour.
The straw hat that has travelled far
is there in the closet of wooden

hangers, hems unravelling;
and the baggy jacket, some buttons gone:
once it was fashionable,

now it is dated like the Aran-shawl
and the shirt with flounces,
frayed like a flag of surrender.

Gifts

1. Gillette

We were not yet wideawake.
My morning skin against the nape
of your neck was rough and bristled

—like sandpaper, you said. So later
in the supermarket, along with other necessities,
you chose for me a gift of razor-blades.

shaving soap: then through the foam
the strokes of the thin steel
gave my face a glabrous, newborn patina.

2. Chanel

The bottle of fragrance
brought back from France
is waiting to be opened and daubed on
just under your ears
and at the base of your throat.

A familiar scent that leaves its trace
and stays when you're gone.
Like a ghost in the wardrobe,
tangled in all your garments,
the silk of a blouse,
the wool of a winter cardigan.

Honeymoon on Achill

It was one more honeymoon day
in the west, God-given and glazed
by a shimmering luminescence.

A day so beautiful it banished
the in-from-the-Atlantic mist
and took us where no-one had ever lived.

We walked in the opposite direction
to the seacrests glinting like a jeweller's
window: walked and walked

through a haze of heat that scorched
bouquets of heather and the scattered
homesteads with all they needed

for the quiet life. On the map of Achill
our travel-path was almost straight
through a bog bereft of shade, an outland

with nowhere to take refuge.
No village between the one we left
and the one at the end of our forward march.

Wicklow Gap

Eventually we turn
from Beethoven's *Ode to Joy*
to his *Grosse Fugue.*
It happens later in life,
on an afternoon of winter blues.
Together we are in a room
where afternoon light catches the dust
and makes it ethereal.
You are reading a book of traveller's tales
from the Age of Steam.
I am looking through the years we keep
in photographs, the halcyon days
when as sweethearts lit from within
we strolled the promenade
and People's Park
or sat as close as we could in the back
of the country bus for a drive
up through the Wicklow Gap.

Vladimir Holan was Right

Vladimir Holan was right:
the kitchen is the best place to be
with its coffee aroma, brewing tea,
prattle of the family and purr

of the icebox working its alchemy.
Stored away in its clammy shadows
are shining apples from Adam's garden,
cherries from Argentina.

A place of healing and mending
and clemency when we confess,
where the only empress is the empress
of wonders that never cease.

At the table of drawn-out pleasures,
wars were fought, you read my thoughts,
black headlines were passed between us.
It is here that daybreak makes its first appearance

and tenebrous evening through steamed windows.
Here that we have been talkative,
silent, amorous; pale as consommé,
rosy as ripe tomatoes.

Figment

Family cars, hanging baskets
colour the avenues and cul-de-sacs
where we came upon the urban fox

ravenous amid the bloated bin-bags,
pilfering the bounty of the black sacks.
Returning from an evening

out with friends, we stopped,
thinking it was a stray dog but Reynard
darted off, vanished like some figment

through railings with rust-spots,
back to his hermitage, back to his Eden
in the weedy undergrowth.

Each night he comes in the ghost hours.
Hungry belly, hungry mouth,
prowling the holy ground.

In God's Ballroom

When you call from a timezone that is distant
you could be on the spice routes,
in the salt mines or some place that skipped
the Age of Enlightenment.

Perhaps you are the interloper
in a holy temple or on the outskirts
of a Third World shantytown
that yearns for justice.

But no, you are high on a mountain,
in God's ballroom
where there are nights of dancing
and many kisses under the mirror-ball
that blindingly dazzles tango-partners
and those who *Cha-Cha*.

The Mirror Tent

for Elish and Gerry

Some have arrived from the river's opposite
side, over the footsloggers' bridge.
Others made Homeric journeys
and crossed the earth. Now we are all here:
the giver of Allah's blessing, the apostle
and emissary of Christ's new testament.

Girls from the east move graciously.
Their colours make it a carnival evening.
There is a truce between all trades:
the singers who perform spiritual chant
and cabaret song; the piper who plays
from his repertoire, *Slievenamon.*

The maestro with his Arabian drum
beats out a rhythm for the tasselled dancer
shimmying and shaking her hips
so that all eyes are on her
and her doppelganger who slips from mirror
to mirror in the mirror-tent.

He Who Treads the Boards

There is a scene where he who treads the boards
is artlessly rhetorical.
— Elizabeth Bishop

With his beguiling voice he has practiced cadence:
the whisper, the shout, change of tone
and change of pace: this actor
who hoards his accolades in a travelling bag.

A brooding Hamlet, a sonorous Vanya,
the blood vision in a Greek tragedy.
On the players' stage, soft-lit he makes entrances,
exits; the quick change from pathos to rage.

Master of silence and master of speech,
of the strut and the dying fall,
of anxiety, inertia and contradictions.

He is like a priest before his congregation,
this actor who must endure
judgments, opinions, the analogy with Narcissus.

September Song

Autumn has come stripping the trees
to make them look like an army in defeat.
Soon everything will appear bereft,
even the girls on the street in décolletage
and canal swans nesting by the side of the bridge:
A pair of them in a swan-marriage,
schooled to be faithful companions.

Roads are brimming with slow-motion traffic
going out of the city, home to the foothills,
to time in the garden pulling weeds,
the Hollywood epic on late-night TV:
the one with the long list of etceteras
scrolled in haste before we turn over
in the double bed of brass reflections.

FOUR

Another Evening in the West

Another evening in the west,
in front of the weather map
that tells us tomorrow will be fine.

Tonight behind smoked glass
porter-taps fill every chalice.
For the last excuse-me dance

the fiddle and accordion commingle
like a couple holding hands.
There is discourse, banter, the *lingua*

franca of men with five o'clock shadows,
whiskey breaths and peaked caps
sideways on their heads.

The women who are garrulous
wear lipstick, damson-red
that makes their lips look overripe.

At closing time they will walk from here
like dumb-show marionettes,
tipsy after another evening in the west.

In Drumcliff Churchyard

where we stopped to find the epitaph,
it seemed just right that we were lost
in rain that pounded the car bonnet

and sounded like a horseman passing by,
his destination further on where sea-wreck
and sand-castle each cast a cracked shadow

and the bruising touch of wind on grass
changed it to a green as dark
as the camouflage of the military
on Border duty, trying hard not to be seen.

New Motorway

From the new motorway we saw our Ararat.
The mountains of South Leinster
blanked with snow that stayed for days
in the clefts and moraines of the high ground
where the whole city becomes a panorama
and the bay in the distance is the last shelter
before the shipping-lanes, before Wales and its peaks.

We passed on the way the wayside pines
and playing fields churned to a quagmire of mud.
The new motorway has its own Bridge of Sighs,
the pedestrian flyover that lights up at dusk
like the spaceship that comes at the end of *ET,*
the spectacular scene that made us weep
with its intimations of a wiser world.

Boyne Tomb

They were proud of the wonders
they worked, the Boyne people
who built this mound,
who hauled kerb-stone and megalith
to the higher ground.
This ancient mound was built
on an upland ridge, whereabouts
of the scribe whose hieroglyphic-code
is undecipherable still.

Until short days of advent
when the sun makes tracks
of quite exact illumination,
the souterrain is lit
by bare electric light
by which we see the way ahead
into the chamber of changeable truth,
empty like the sepulchre in Jerusalem.

'Mise Éire'

Easter lilies are out for Easter Sunday.
The last veterans are gone,
the procession of them that used to gather
mingling local argot and schoolbook grammar.

This mid-April morning, between oration
and oration, we hear once more Ó Riada's
back-stiffening threnody,
familiar, as if it was written yesterday.

The billowy tricolour, hoisted in honour
of a time that fell out of history,
looks as if it is only part of the pomp, pageant fodder.

Between the colonnades of the Post Office
they are selling laminates of poets, pedagogues:
the seven back from purdah.

Plunkett, Clarke, McDermott, Ceannt,
Connolly, Pearse, MacDonagh.

Path Through Life

The barns are stuffed.
The smoke above the world
comes from the burning chaff.
Days are humdrum or else they are full
of trouble at the family table.

The beasts shift in their dung.
They sleep on straw, sequestered
in the fog-house of their hibernation.
The birds are busy darting down
to pick what morsels can be found
in the shaved corn meadow:
small crumbs of harvest spillage
or on the harbour wall, sprat-fish.

In the small village of waging tongues
the old ideas are still the ones
that matter and are learned by heart
so that the living can carry on
and take what comes on the path through life.

Lough Derg

Years ago I spent a sleepless night
among sleepwalkers ready to renounce
the world, the flesh, the devil.

It was all Dantesque,
circling and circling the purgatorial beds
in the wet wind and chill from the lake,
to the chant of mingling strangers
ready to make a new beginning.

Black tea, black bread
was the sustenance we were given.
In the first light at five o'clock
the shore appeared out of the dark.
It made us think we were close to God
years ago on Lough Derg.

Free State

for John McGahern

Saying *Goodbye* at the airport
you speak of destinations far from home,
of distance that wearies
the jet-age traveller
and the long journey ahead
through all the beautiful cities.
Cities like stories waiting to be read.

But I am happy
motoring through the Free State,
the Glebe Road where O'Carolan dragged his harp,
the hilly landscape where on some days
the lake is radiant and still.
On other days it is like a page
of thumbprints, dull and marked
by cloud-shadow
and the meadow-dust of Leitrim.

The German Graveyard in Glencree

In the German graveyard in Glencree
we take a look around and then we leave
the dead to their togetherness,
their vale of quarry rock, waterfall, precipice.

It is bare except for a laurel wreath,
the grotto that echoes as soon as we cross
the threshold. We crouch
to find the names of those interred.

Beneath heather that awaits springtime
resurrection, undisturbed in their oasis
the dead find peace and a state of grace.
Here where water flows ceremonially
and makes the sound of healing.

Flood

It must have happened while
my eyes were closed.
The river poured into the town.
The moon turned up the volume of the tides.

Soon sandbags were stacked
like the trench-defences
in *All Quiet On The Western Front.*
Floodwater burst into back alleys

and bits of ground where people
were born, lived, died.
It came through the hall where someone
was singing about *Apple Blossom Time.*

Like the fire in Alexandria,
it surpassed our understanding:
everything destroyed
or made unrecognisable: books

and boutique dresses;
the shopkeeper's supply of bread and cheese
and wine, his jars of honey
and the tailor's dummy
like a backstroke swimmer in the Nile.

Fairground Attractions

Tomorrow they will disassemble
the fairground attractions: the shooting-gallery
where every shot is counted, the merry-go-round
that tonight keeps pace with the wheel of fortune

speeding up, slowing down. In the fortune-teller's tent
Madame's sixth sense tells her everything
once she hears the click of coins in the silver dish.

The passage through which families pass
is made of looking-glass that makes them seem
like the Cubist figures of Picasso and Braque.

And bearing the light of magic lanterns
the ghost train runs on its little track
into the other world of shivers in the darkness.

The Lying-In Hospital

A star in the east stands over
the lying-in hospital, the delivery suite
where mothers and daughters,
fathers and sons first meet.

Propped up on hospital pillows
the lactating daughter breastfeeds
the new child in her arms
that the streets outside are waiting to harm.

Same streets as those I wandered
as a child sent out for milk
into the stargazer's night of bliss,
where frost already hard has settled
on the graveyard of Huguenot families.
The weavers who came for sanctuary.

Linnet

I went out to taste the calm
that evening brings - the armistice.
From the wooden bridge
I watched strangers in oilskin jackets
steer into the mooring, in for the night
to that out-of-the-way place
of respite from the human struggle.

And walking farther on I found a church
and churchyard, treeless
on the upward side of town,
both there since the time of the curse
that caused the first language to vanish.
The headstone narratives
of thinned-out words stood untouched

for a hundred years.
And Yeats's linnet sang in the bushes,
a lamentation for the newly-dead.
With dank breath the weather
came down the mountain to make walls weep
and lay a cold cheek on the vestiges
of cloister ground and clerestories.

Sea Pictures

We stayed in a house of sea pictures.
A house with a view of the sea itself,
of a pier that stood in the tides,

crumbling to nothing, in need of a Midas-touch.
Sometime we had on our backs a sunny breeze.
Sometimes a gale chased our heels.

The cottage doors were always open,
exhaling heat from kitchen fires,
allowing the long twilights in.

A fishing village, a lifeboat station:
in summer sandals we took the back roads
between those places,

down to the white strand
where a local Prospero walked his dog,
a terrier chasing a phantom stick.

Or down to the harbour with its oil stain
making a face of Jesus,
its safe haven vacated while the boats

were on the herring-fields or hauling in
the lobster creels that August when
my childish drawings were a homage to the sea.

Singing City

We drove for miles through wet valleys.
Munster valleys we know from poets
and their rhapsodies.

Past the sugar factory and empty dancehall
where the last dancers left their shadows
and the mirror ball hangs like a wintry moon.

From a hillside of upturned earth
a magpie came scudding into our perspective.
One magpie always makes me nervous.

On the passenger side close to the verges
I kept watch on the watchful south
until we arrived in the singing city

where the chimes of bells prevailed
and like the fallen after a battle
broken umbrellas were scattered on Grand Parade.

According to Matthew

Falling sparrows, camels passing
through the eye of a needle.
He speaks in metaphors and riddles.
He is a riddle, the Virgin's Son
who stands to pronounce the blunt one-liners
of the Sermon on the Mount:
Blessed are... Come follow me...

In *The Gospel According to Matthew,*
the version by Pasolini,
Christ the agitator hurries through Galilee
healing the stretcher-borne,
casting away the bread of stone
placed before him in temptation.

Christ in the temple speaks in livid gestures:
upending and taking apart
the tables and tills of the money-lenders.
He sits cross-legged to answer the questions
of potentate and plebeian, or with a stick
writes on the ground, defends the slut against the crowd
with a handful of words quite clear to everyone.

Morning Offerings

They rise up and walk with their beds,
out into a day of doleful countenance.
From the night-shelter dormitories
they break loose, our city nomads.

With an anorak-hood to cover his head,
one looks rough and one is hunched
beneath the rucksack on his shoulders.

Some are young and can improvise.
Some have already devoted a life to the passing
of time—they disappear, turn a corner.

Some to the palace of fruit machines,
some to the pipes at the back of a church.
Others wander into the park to seek a refuge,
find a path of morning offerings.

Creed Room

To the creed room came the newsflash
that mutated into hot metal,
ink on the pages of *Revelation*.

Ricochets from the first shots
in a war of liberation, the silence of weapons
put down on the peace conference table.

First inklings of small earthquakes,
of the pitiless epidemic.
News of the world and reasons to lament

for the innocents crowded into makeshift
mortuaries, for the hostage kept
in a new Gethsemane.

To the creed room came narratives
from the Sea of Tranquility
and the Red Sea shore.

From the frontline and Great Divide
came paragraphs naming places
never mentioned before:

the streets where executioners
gathered stones, where death-chants
conflated to a manic roar.

Comet

for Sheila Wayman

It reappears in our garden of galaxies.
A soul in flight, a soul of ice and dust.
I imagine it, already there on the day
of the first man and the first woman.

And there in the time of Plato
centuries before Christ. It was nameless then
and nameless when in the season
of Roman festivals, it was seen

by shepherds who watched for signs,
who were frightened by the celestial.
Now it returns to blind the new astronomers
whose eyes are upon it, rummaging among the stars.

Printed in the United Kingdom
by Lightning Source UK Ltd.
120031UK00001B/256-273